Att Right Girl

How To Find Your Perfect Girl And Make Her Chase You For A Relationship

By Bruce Bryans

Legal Disclaimer

Although the information in this book may be very useful, it is sold with the understanding that neither the author nor the publisher is engaged in presenting specific psychological, emotional, or sexual advice. Nor is anything in this book intended to be a diagnosis, prescription, recommendation, or cure for any specific kind of psychological, emotional, or sexual problem. Each person has unique needs and this book cannot take these individual differences into account.

ISBN-13: 978-1482549706

ISBN-10: 1482549700

Introduction

Sometimes I think back on how I used to be when I was trying to attract and build relationships with women. It's enjoyable to me because I'm able to see how far I've come and how much I've grown as a man. It gives me a sense of perspective on what's actually important in life and what's not so important; especially when it comes to getting that one dream girl.

I think back on the kinds of women that I used to date and I realize that no matter how gorgeous some of them might have appeared to be on the surface, they all had some sort of emotional baggage or character flaw that would just end up driving me crazy.

I mean, no matter how pretty, cute, fine, or gorgeous she was I just couldn't seem to find a woman who was free from all the "drama" so to speak. In fact, one time it got so bad that I ended up in a relationship with this one girl who was obsessively jealous, manipulative, and a total emotional shipwreck.

It was hell-on-earth.

I remember it so vividly because that's when I began to seriously consider where my life was headed. I started to wonder what kind of man I was if all I seemed to attract were these extremely damaged women. In reality it wasn't a fun time for me, I can remember that much.

Of course, it was kind of fun in the sense that I was playing the field and having a good time, but it was costing me my peace of mind, life success, and long-term happiness. I must actually thank her some day because that experience did help (force) me to want to change the kind of man I was so that I could find a phenomenal, drama-free woman to build a meaningful relationship with.

And you know what?

I soon realized that no matter how beautiful, gorgeous, smart, funny, or sexy a woman was if she didn't have a beautiful CHARACTER, she was a complete waste of my time. I refused to lower my standards and focused on dating highly attractive women who also had hearts of gold.

It became that serious for me.

I eventually determined NOT to date women based solely on physical attractiveness or mutual chemistry alone. I figured out that without a strong character, it was impossible for me to have the kind of relationship that few people ever experience in this world.

I realized that only a woman that embodied things like honesty, sincerity, kindness, loyalty, respect for men, and gracefulness could keep me interested for a very long time. Without these kinds of qualities, no woman could or would be able to build a deeply intimate and powerful relationship with me.

I wanted a woman that embodied that which was good in the world and beautiful IN a woman. I wanted to have the kind of girlfriend that I could carry before kings and queens and she'd be able to fit right in if need be.

In other words, I wanted a woman of <u>noble</u> character.

A woman's character or lack thereof can make or break you.

No matter how strong or in control you think you are as a man, don't be fooled. When you decide to develop a relationship with a woman, she WILL have an influence on you no matter what. This is why it is essential to seek out a woman that has the kind of qualities that will add VALUE to your life. And if she's not adding value to you she's definitely taking it away from you.

You don't want that now do you? Of course not!

If you really want a relationship with a 'Total 10' woman who's drop-dead gorgeous, a blast to be around, and committed to treating you like royalty, you need to learn how to judge a woman's worth by her character instead of just her looks. I'm not saying that outward beauty isn't important, because it is. In fact, for men, it's essential. But don't let her outward appearance determine your level of interest in her.

So if you're currently looking for Ms. Right here's a tip:

Resolve only to date a woman if she possesses the kind of virtuous qualities that you know will add value to your life. By doing this you'll find that you'll become a beacon for high-quality women, simply because you've made a conscious decision to raise your standards.

In fact, make it a declaration and tell yourself often that you only date high-quality, beautiful women who have hearts of gold. Your boldness in setting a standard WILL set you apart from most guys and you'll find yourself assessing a woman based on her actions and behaviors as opposed to her beauty alone.

This will put you in a position of power since you're no longer the kind of guy that's always trying to get a woman's approval. Now, you're seeing if a woman has the kind of character that YOU approve of. This makes you out to be a leader in her eyes.

In the pages that follow, I'm going to describe a 'Total Package' woman and why having her as a girlfriend will add far more success and happiness to your life.

This kind of woman thinks very differently from the average woman when it comes to dating men and she's quite picky when selecting a potential mate. A woman like this is not only looking for Mr. Right, but a Mr. Right that fits her subconscious image of the ideal man. She has a lot of options and very high standards when it comes to men, because she knows she's worth it.

By learning how to recognize a high-quality woman, you'll be in a much better position to attract her into your life. Also, by becoming just as selective as she is when it comes to a potential mate, you'll become far more attractive to her.

The first step to getting what you want is to know what you want, and the second step to getting what you want is to DESERVE what you want. This is the secret to attracting the woman of your dreams, because if you don't become highly selective when it comes to dating women, you'll continue to fall prey to low-quality women and lackluster relationships.

Tables Of Contents

CHAPTER 1:
Know What You Want And Deserve What You Want

Increasing Your Standards Gets You Better Results

Dating an average woman that isn't a good match for you or who isn't highly attracted to you or interested in adding value to your life is actually WORSE than being single. Ending up with a woman who isn't compatible is a sentence to a life filled with misery, boredom, and continuous conflict and frustration.

Believe me on this one, you don't want to start a romantic relationship with anyone that doesn't meet your high standards. In the past I've tried to date women on the basis of "hotness" alone, and the results have been nothing short of frustrating.

Chemistry and compatibility are extremely important when choosing an ideal girlfriend. But it doesn't stop there.

In order for you to attract and choose the BEST woman for you, one who has the 'Total Package', you actually have to increase your standards, and clarify exactly what qualities in a woman are most important to you.

By clarifying what you want you'll begin to filter out low-quality women from your dating experience and make room for superior women. As soon as you make the decision to ONLY date women that meet certain standards, you actually become a beacon for higher-quality women.

You'll 'beat the odds' so to speak, when it comes to finding and dating higher-quality women by refusing to settle for women that do not add the kind of value to your life that you know you deserve.

And there's the magic word right there…

Deserve.

You must know what you want, and you must believe that you deserve to have it. When these two things converge…then and only then will you begin to see a major difference in the kinds of women that take notice of YOU first. This is a much better position to be in instead of you always having to chase women in the first place.

A 'Total Package' Woman Will Make Your Life MUCH Easier

Building an honest, open, loving, and trust-filled relationship with a woman that is HIGHLY INVESTED AND INTERESTED in YOU is VERY different from trying to build a relationship with a woman who is not.

This is important and should not be taken lightly. Why? Because many of the tools and techniques I suggest in the final section of this book will either make or break your relationship based on this premise.

If the woman you're with is VERY attracted to you and wants nothing more than to stand by your side for the long-haul, then these techniques will help you to anchor that attraction and transform it into a powerful force for developing a passionate, blissful relationship. You won't have to use mind games and persuasive tricks to keep her happy, and you won't have to resort

3

to wasting vast amounts of time or money to keep her interested in you.

On the other hand, if the woman you're with is NOT very attracted or compatible with you from the outset, using these tools and techniques will make your relationship a one-sided affair where you're doing all of the giving and she's not. This is NOT the kind of scenario you want for your life.

This is why it is extremely important for you to choose a woman that is right for you, who is also very attracted to you, and who's interested in taking things to the next level with you. Trying to force an uninterested woman into a deep, harmonious relationship is like trying to force a round peg into a square hole. It just won't work.

This is why it's so important for you to choose a high-quality woman from the outset. This will allow you build a solid foundation for a successful relationship.

On Finding Miss Right

So you're on your way to becoming the kind of man that can attract the woman that is right for you. You're doing the best you can to be the best version of yourself at this particular point of your own personal development, and you can't help but wonder...where or when is she going to show up?

Patience my friend, she will come. If you build it (your character and personality)...she will come.

4

But if you want to increase your chances of finding that special girl, you're going to have to get outside of your comfort zone.

Often.

Just about anything that you want to achieve or accomplish in this life that is out of the ordinary will require you to get outside of your comfort zone. And the same applies for finding that special girl.

Obviously doing the things you've been doing for years hasn't been working out so well, so why not shake things up a bit?

And have you really sat down and asked yourself:

"What kind of activities does the kind of woman I want to be with engage in, and where exactly can I find her? What is she passionate about and what are her values and personal beliefs?"

Asking yourself these questions may quickly narrow down your choices of where and how to look.

For instance, it's highly unlikely that you'll find a high-quality, relationship-material girlfriend in a strip club. I mean, seriously now, let's think about it. Do you really think that you'll attract the woman of your dreams (assuming you're looking for the classy type) in a strip club?

This is highly unlikely.

Use common sense and really think about it. And when you ask yourself that question, you must take into account the kind of activities that interest you as well.

Where do the kinds of women that you're really interested in hang out? And what similar interests might you share with this kind of woman?

You want to get outside of your comfort zone, but you don't want to get outside of who you are and what you're all about.

For instance, if you're into travel, exploration, and adventure, then it's highly unlikely that you'll find a fulfilling relationship with a woman whose greatest idea of fun and adventure is a shopping trip to the mall.

You won't be very happy in the long run.

So with this in mind, try to be as honest with yourself as possible by asking first what it is that you want, and secondly what kinds of activities does your ideal woman engage in?

Defining the Woman of Your Dreams

Sit down someplace quiet and visualize what kind of relationship you'd really like to be in with your ideal woman and begin thinking about the qualities she possesses that would truly make you happy in a relationship.

As your vision takes shape, write down at least ten things that you want in your dream girl. Be painfully honest with yourself so that you're honest with the women you come across as well. It may seem harsh, and even downright impossible to narrow your wants down, but few guys have the courage to even try.

Remember that you shouldn't set limits on yourself, but you MUST focus on what will make YOU happy instead of what will impress your friends, build your ego, or make you feel important.

Knowing what will make you happy means that you also know what will make you unhappy. So don't put anything on your list if it isn't authentic.

And there's something else that I want you to keep in mind...

When everyone is your customer, no one is your customer.

What this means is that if you don't define what it is you want by narrowing down your options, you'll always get what it is you don't really want. When it comes to attracting the right woman, she'll never show up on your radar because you'll have no idea what she really looks like or how she behaves.

So it's in your best interest to think about what you want and define your "customer."

I should also note that this is in no way, shape or form, about finding the perfect specimen of a woman. This is about being honest with yourself about what you truly want in a highly compatible mate.

What usually happens is that we settle for a woman (usually because of fear) and over the course of several months or years we end up trying to change them to fit our list. And believe me, whether or not you actually sit down to make a list by writing it out, you DO have a list, even if it's deep inside your subconscious mind.

When we're finally honest with ourselves (after realizing this person isn't what I really wanted and trying to change them to fit my list is futile) we end up calling the whole thing off. Then the process only continues with someone else while we hope for different results.

It may seem harsh to be so specific in making a list about what it is you want in a woman, but it's even harsher to try and make someone else fit your ideal of a "perfect" woman.

You don't have to share your list with anyone. Just make it, stick it someplace private, and refer to it often to keep that mental picture of what it is you really want.

When you meet a woman you're really attracted to, pull out that list and see if they measure up. If they do - great, if they don't - great, because you can move on instead of wasting both her time and yours.

So be a man about it, and make your list.

Choose a Woman That Compliments Your Life

When you get the guts to not only create, but also stick to your list, only look for a potential mate within the natural course of your life's journey. This includes things like your work, recreations, hobbies, etc. This will make the potential high-quality women you meet far more compatible with you and way more attracted to you in the long run.

The cliché is that opposites attract, but I haven't come across any proof that says opposites enjoy enriching long-term relationships. The reality is couples who are more compatible stay together longer and enjoy far more intimacy in a relationship.

So think about your life goals, your passions, and your interests, and focus on dating quality women that "fit" with you in those areas. Don't start things off on the wrong foot by trying to attract a woman you have next to nothing in common with.

And always, ALWAYS, go for chemistry and compatibility over sex appeal and "hotness" alone. Building an enjoyable relationship will be tough work, so don't make it an uphill battle for yourself by focusing on physical beauty alone as opposed to what's on the inside.

Trust in Your List

The last thing you should consider when looking for "The One" is to stop looking for "The One" and simply trust in your list. You must do this wholeheartedly, because the more detached you are from the process, the faster it happens.

I know, it doesn't make sense, and in all honesty it's difficult to explain, but bear with me…

It kind of works like this, if you're not "looking for a relationship" you won't appear needy when you do come across a great woman. Your laid-back attitude will make you appear like more of a catch. It's a paradox, but it's one that works extremely well for getting you what you really want.

If you go into every single interaction with a woman thinking that "she could be it", you'll put an enormous amount of pressure on yourself AND on her, and you may just end up ruining your chances for something special to develop on its own. So learn to go with the flow, work on becoming a better man, and trust in your list knowing that your ideal woman is probably more on the lookout for you than you are for her.

Why Most Guys FAIL to Attract Their Ideal Woman

Many guys fail to attract the right girl because of fear. They fear being alone the rest of their lives or they fear commitment. Whatever the fear is, often times it causes people to either settle for a relationship that barely fulfills them (if at all), or they completely miss out on many potentially fulfilling relationships with extraordinary women.

So make the list, because whether you believe it or not, everyone has one. Everyone might not have it written down, but they do have one. Write yours down, and refer to it often until you've memorized EXACTLY what it is you're looking for. Why? Because your mind is an extremely powerful goal-achieving machine, so use it to your advantage.

The reason why we make the list is to avoid settling for someone and then trying to change her to fit our list. In reality, it's much better to have an idea of what you're looking for. It's about knowing yourself and getting to truly know the core of another person. Many relationships fail as couples try to force one another to conform to their standards based on false expectations.

Making the list and following the steps for finding and attracting your ideal woman will help you to make better dating decisions and will actually save you from unnecessary stress and frustration. You'll be able to filter potential mates much better, and you'll naturally grow as a person simply because you'll begin to subconsciously develop the qualities that will be attractive to your ideal woman.

By being honest with yourself you'll have a better chance at attracting a great girlfriend since you'll be thinking and acting with more integrity in your dating life. And you'll also avoid hurting yourself and others in the long-run.

How to Create Your Own Luck

There are some things that you can do to help yourself to get lucky if you're trying to find the right woman for you. Luckily for you, it's the kind of luck that can be created.

Here are a few ideas that will help you as long as you take some action on them. These are all simple suggestions for the main purpose of getting you to take bold action and get out of your comfort zone, as this is exactly where you're going to find that one of a kind woman who can have a great impact on your life.

Although some of these suggestions are to get you out of your comfort zone, things should never feel forced. Interacting with her in a new setting should almost feel "natural", as if you were, "in the right place, at the right time".

11

Get Out of Your Comfort Zone

That's it.

This has nothing to do with you being an introvert or an extrovert, simply go out more, get a life, and socialize with other humans. Where to go? Wherever there are other humans, of course. Although, you might prefer to spend time with people who share similar interests with you or who are doing things that may become interesting to you later.

You normally don't hear much about people finding "The One" while sitting at home watching other people go out to meet other people in those sitcoms that we all tend to indulge in now and then.

And don't get me started on "reality" TV.

But anyway, let's move on.

Sitting down on your couch waiting for the right woman to fall through the roof doesn't happen, not even in the movies. How else are you going to be in the right place at the right time to attract your ideal woman if you're never in any place at any time?

So go out and meet people. Get out of your home and hang out with people. Try new things with new people and increase your circle of relationships. You'll get to create more memories with your friends, or even gain some new friends in the process.

This is an excellent way to network, and you may end up stumbling upon a pretty phenomenal relationship with a spectacular woman who's actually been looking and waiting for you to SHOW UP.

Keep a Positive Mental Attitude

There is a certain universal law that states that more comes to the person who already has. The same applies with love and romance. Do you radiate optimism as a man? Are you a fun and radiant person to be around? If not, you're probably going to have a tougher time attracting any woman at all.

I'm not saying that you have to be bouncing off the walls when you get into a social setting. All I'm saying is that being a killjoy won't win you any votes with high-quality women.

If you want to find romance, find ways to enjoy your life more as you are now. Become so wrapped up in enjoying your life and being a great person to hang out with that people will want to go out of their way to be in your presence - especially the opposite sex.

This works well when trying to find the right woman that can enhance the quality of your life. As you begin to naturally become a more fun-filled and joyful person to be around, you may eventually stumble upon a romantic relationship with a woman who has simply fallen in love with your zest for life.

Begin to live a passionate and adventurous life now. Don't wait for someone else to create it for you. Build the feelings of a life of passion and purpose so that you can more easily attract the right woman to you.

Follow Your Passions

Yes, it sounds weird, but let me explain.

By following your passions you set yourself up for new experiences and new relationships. These new experiences and new relationships can lead to you finding the kind of woman that you've always dreamed of being with.

Following your passions means doing the things that bring you the most happiness and fulfillment. You should do more of the things that captivate your attention and give you a sense of rapture and flow.

Do the things that fill your life with meaning as a man.

Joseph Campbell, a mythologist, philosopher and academic used to tell his students to "follow your bliss". He told them to pursue those things that energized them, where they lost a sense of time and they could do it all day. He told them that life rewards those who follow their bliss. And even in my own personal experience, the more I've followed this piece of advice the more success and happiness I seem to stumble across.

The word for this is 'serendipity.'

Why is this important when trying to find the ideal woman? Simple, relationships are not that difficult to find and create, but fulfilling relationships are much more rare and unique.

So by doing more of the things that you love to do, you end up attracting more loving and authentic relationships with people who admire you for who you are. In this way, it is possible to find the right woman for you, and develop a romantic relationship that truly fulfills you as a man.

You're not trying to be anyone or anything but the happiest and most enthusiastic and authentic version of yourself. And that's all that anyone really wants. To be in a romantic and fulfilling relationship with someone who simply loves them for them.

CHAPTER 2:
How To Recognize And Select A High-Quality Girlfriend

The One Rare Quality of a Phenomenal Woman

So what really makes that one special girl so rare and irreplaceable? Well for starters, one of the most attractive things about a woman is her ability to influence a man without the need to be forceful. Any intelligent, self-directed man would tell you that he would prefer to be influenced by a woman he loved rather than forced.

As men we enjoy feeling a sense of power that comes from being in charge, and yet only a handful of women truly understand this fact and use this knowledge to help us to make better decisions. This assumes of course, that she's the kind of woman who's interested in helping you to become a better man.

But most women often think that to get a man's attention or to get him to do something will require endless amounts of nagging, argument, or some other kind of ineffective behavior. This couldn't be further from the truth.

In reality, most of us guys are more easily influenced by something else that a woman possesses. Not only is it a persuasive quality, but it is also extremely attractive to us. It is one of those qualities that make a woman highly attractive to a man, and you should consciously be on the lookout for it.

This simple, subtle thing can be called *feminine grace*, and it allows a woman to bring out her full inner beauty and elegance. Any woman who possesses such a trait is a likely candidate for being your future Miss Right.

Why Graceful Women Are in High-Demand

Gracefulness makes a woman desirable, sexy, and powerful. When a woman has feminine grace, she not only becomes much more attractive to the opposite sex, but she lives her life with more purpose and passion. It is this very passion and enthusiasm for life that attracts us to such women. It's women like this that possess a certain sexiness that we cannot deny.

You may have read stories of women throughout history that men have gone to war for. You've probably read about women that have started wars and ended them, or women that have influenced men to do great things, to go on great journeys, or to make great discoveries.

These were the kinds of women that had influence over even the most powerful of men. And the sole reason for that is because of the feminine gracefulness that they possessed which attracts high-quality men towards them.

A woman's power of influence and attractiveness when it comes to men goes beyond the physical into the realm of the spiritual. It is her feminine essence that makes men magnetically drawn to her, as well as an inspiration for other women.

Another way of explaining this x-factor is with one word…

Class.

I'm sure you've come across those women who seemed to grab your attention EVEN when they weren't necessarily your "type" or even "drop dead" gorgeous. It was just something else that they had that made you want to be around them and enjoy their company.

This, my friend, was a woman's feminine charm at work. You should become aware of this essence as you consciously seek it out in the woman you want.

Keep in mind however, that feminine grace isn't merely about how a woman acts; it has more to do with the passionate and purposeful way in which she lives her life. It's not so much about her charm alone, but it encompasses the totality of who she is and how she exudes her confidence in the way she dresses, the way she speaks, how she treats those around her, and how she treats men.

She loves who she is and she embraces her femininity. She is dignified and has the utmost respect for a good man.

I repeat…she is dignified and has the utmost respect for a good man.

This is the kind of woman who knows how to show restraint, who is in control of herself, and who displays humility and discretion. In short, she's a lady, and she expects to be treated like one.

And if, by comparison, a high-quality man has a character of chivalry and honor, then a high-quality woman displays a character of grace and poise.

This is how she illustrates her virtue and her nobility.

Grace, Romance, and Seduction

We may not be outright romantic creatures by nature, but a woman can influence you to be more romantic by using her feminine ways to entice and captivate you. It's a strange feeling in which you'll WANT to take care of her and treat her like a queen. You'd fight for her if the situation called for it, and you'd gladly make the sacrifices necessary to ensure her happiness.

The idea of romance encompasses the idea of the chivalrous man. And nothing can trigger this powerful feeling in a man like a woman who has fully embraced her feminine strength by developing her queen-like gracefulness.

Only a noble woman can fully create this feeling in the chivalrous man. So keep this in mind as you begin filtering out the kinds of women that you really want to date and build a meaningful, long-term relationship with.

She Radiates Inner Confidence

You want to be with the kind of woman that is comfortable with the fact that she is, inherently, a woman. A woman who exudes feminine grace is quite comfortable with her feminine nature. She's confident in herself and embraces the fact that she's a woman, and she'll want nothing more from you than to be THE

MAN that she can give her respect, support, and intimacy.

A high-quality woman of grace can communicate without words. In essence, not only is she aware of whom she is, but she is fully in-tuned with what she is. She knows and loves the fact that she is a woman, and she loves to be around a man who embraces his masculinity.

Read that last sentence again…

When a graceful woman enters the room, we simply know. She doesn't need to say anything or even reveal her presence with words. Her very essence is magnetic. She communicates with her body language in a way that says that she is comfortable with her sexuality, and that she expects to be appreciated and adored. She appreciates the fact that she is the fairer of the sexes, and she lives passionately.

The graceful woman is CONFIDENT in her sexuality as a feminine creature. So with that in mind, wouldn't it make sense that such a woman would be highly attracted to a man that is CONFIDENT in his sexuality as a masculine being?

It's all a part of the game of attraction and it's based solely on the polarizations of the masculine and the feminine energies. Mature masculinity cannot help but to attract mature femininity. In other words, the more you develop yourself as a man, the more attractive you will be to a high-quality woman.

What a Graceful Woman Means to You

What a graceful woman desires more than anything is to be appreciated for the fact that she is a woman, and as a woman she desires one thing from her masculine equivalent:

She desires the freedom to express her true femininity completely. She wants to be with a man who is strong enough to allow her to be irrational, emotional, loving, desiring, helpful, and every other quality that a woman may want to express. And she wants to be with a man who makes her feel like a woman, because of his masculine presence. She will deeply respect a man who compels her to live with passion and purpose.

The graceful woman wants freedom from masculine responsibilities and masculine expectations. She desires freedom to display her emotions as they come to her, and the freedom to express her sexuality in her own unique way with modesty and enthusiasm.

The more she senses your masculine and chivalrous nature, the more attracted she will be to you. This is all part of the game of romantic seduction. And what can possibly be more romantic than the game of the woman as the graceful damsel and you as her chivalrous knight?

High-Quality Women Treat Their Men Like Kings

I'm about to show you exactly how a good woman will and should treat you. I really want you to end up choosing the kind of woman that can help make your life much more enriching in the long run. Remember to keep this idea in mind the next time you come across a potential candidate.

Are you ready for it? Yes? Good, because here it is:

Every man, no matter what his creed, culture, or calling, wants to be treated like a king. And if you have taken the time to develop yourself into a more well-rounded man of high-character, then you deserve to be with a woman that recognizes your worth and your true potential.

Yet, there are women out there that simply don't have a clue. Though they mean well, some of them just do not know how to keep a quality guy interested in them simply because they're unaware (or unwilling) to treat him the way he should be treated.

You don't want to end up with a woman like this.

What you want is the kind of woman who knows how to treat a real man. No one is perfect of course, but always consider the way a woman treats you the next time you're interacting with her. Or better yet, notice the way she treats the men in her life.

When you come across a woman that you might consider great 'girlfriend material', observe how she treats her father, her brothers, her cousins, and male friends. This is a dead giveaway for how she might treat you in the future.

She Provides Unwavering Loyalty and Support

Kings would often go to great lengths to ensure that those he serves as are unwaveringly loyal to him and the kingdom. The same applies with how you should treat a good woman and how she should be treating you.

Let's face it; the world can be a pretty negative and stressful place at times. There's no denying this fact. But a man should feel at peace in his own home and in his relationship. His home should be his haven and he shouldn't feel as if he can't <u>trust</u> the woman he's with, no matter what other good qualities she may appear to have.

A good woman will display an unwavering loyalty and support to you if she believes that you are more than capable of leading her and making her life much more rich and fulfilling.

She should communicate to you through her actions that she desires to serve and love you unconditionally, and only you, so long as you're being the man that you're supposed to be. And you should be able to place your confidence in her to be there for you, even when things aren't working out in your favor and you're down on your luck.

This point can't be stressed enough. The more you can feel completely safe and open with a woman, the

25

more you will learn to depend on her for support and serve her dutifully as a man should.

You'll want to know without a shadow of doubt that you can place your confidence in her, and that you can pour your all into the relationship. And of course you know that a good woman will not lie to you, cheat on you, or steal from you.

Seriously, these things go without saying, but there's more:

She won't be petty and malicious to you especially when you're down.

She isn't the type who complains about your less redeeming qualities to her friends, family, and co-workers.

She should never insult or downplay your importance to others, especially your children.

She keeps your relationship issues and arguments private, unless of course it's professional help.

She will want to resolve relationship conflicts as quickly as possible, and would rather not end the day being angry or upset with you.

She's open and honest with you, and is willing to do her part to build and sustain a harmonious relationship.

Every man sees himself as a king in his home and relationship, as every woman should see herself as a confident and capable queen. Believe it or not, the way a woman treats you has more to do with you than it does with her.

The way you treat yourself and the way you treat her will have a great affect on her level of respect for you and just how attracted to you she can become.

With this in mind, you should make your woman feel like a queen by communicating your loyalty and sincerity to her and by showing her your appreciation in romantic ways. Encourage and cultivate her feminine spirit and she'll continuously give you her utmost respect as she stands by your side with love and loyalty.

But above all, as a man you MUST have high standards for yourself and your woman and low tolerance for dishonesty or lack of integrity from you, her, or anyone else for that matter. It may sound strange, but if you can communicate this to a woman early on in your interactions with her, you would have set a firm foundation in place for building a successful, drama free relationship.

She is a Thoughtful, Proactive Lover

A proactive lover is simply someone who understands the needs and desires of their significant other, and goes out of their way to ensure that these needs and desires are met consistently. If you want to find a great woman to share your time and resources with, then make sure that she's a proactive lover.

For example, do you like football? A thoughtful and proactive woman will want to do what she can to ensure that you're happy while engaging in one of your favorite past times. She'll be willing to support your love for it by going out of her way to bring more happiness into your life.

She doesn't have to fake an interest in the sport, but gestures as simple as making sure that you don't miss your favorite teams play, surprising you with tickets, or even serving you and your buddies some food while you watch the game won't go unnoticed.

Think about it.

If you work at a job that might be stressful, what might a thoughtful woman do to ensure that your castle (home) is pleasant, peaceful, and free from all kinds of conflict? She might have your favorite drink ready for you when you get home with your favorite music playing in the background to help you relax. She might even want to give you a massage to help you release some of your tension.

What if you travel a lot or work at a potentially dangerous profession? Maybe she might want to ensure that the time she spends with you are especially memorable and beautiful.

These are general examples, but if she treats you like a king, you'll be more likely to return to your woman with an "I can't wait to see her" attitude. And the more you give to her, the more you'll receive from the relationship as well.

Of course, there should be balance in everything. Remember, it's not about her giving you everything you ask for, it's about the fact that she's willing to cater to your inner most needs and desires.

In other words, she's the kind of woman that looks out for your entire well-being, and she ensures that the quality of your life has been increased simply because she's now in it.

How She Adds to Your Success and Happiness

"No man is happy or complete without the modifying influence of the right woman." These are the words spoken by Napoleon Hill in his best-belling personal development classic, *Think And Grow Rich*. These words illustrate just how much influence a woman can and WILL have over you, and this is why it's essential that you select the RIGHT woman from the start.

A high-quality woman who's perfect for you will add to your success and happiness because of the *inner gifts* she has to offer you. In reality, these are the aspects about a woman that will have the greatest affect on your mental and emotional well-being.

I'm going to list what I believe are the most valuable qualities to look out for. So keep them in mind as you search for your ideal woman.

She'll Appreciate Your Strengths

First of all, you want to be with a woman who will make you feel as if you make a difference in her world. We've all watched the movies and read the books with powerful masculine heroes in it. And you've seen how women who deeply appreciate them both for their character and their achievements usually accompany these heroic men.

Unfortunately, many women these days cannot comprehend the importance of simply allowing a man to be a man. Men have egos, usually large ones. There's no getting around this fact.

A woman who understands this is one that will make you happy since she'll understand how to carefully cater to your ego.

No, she won't worship you, but she will give you credit where it's DUE.

She will respect you when you attempt your best, even if you fail.

In fact, this is the most important aspect of choosing a woman to build a relationship with. She MUST show signs that she RESPECTS the men in her life.

For starters, watch the way she treats strangers, both men and women, but especially men. Does she flirt with other guys in front of you, or at all? Does she display manners and common courtesy to others? And even more importantly, how does she treat her father, brothers, and male friends?

Observe how she treats the men in her life and you'll catch a glimpse of your future with her. Does she constantly berate them for their shortcomings or is she patient, tenderhearted, and grateful for the things they do right?

No woman can hide her true behavior for too long.

Also keep in mind that a good woman will make you feel as if your presence matters to her. She'll know how to communicate her appreciation for just having you around. And just having you around is more than enough to make her happy and fulfilled.

You're not looking for a woman to help increase your self-esteem here. That's mostly YOUR job, but you are looking for a woman that can build up the best that's already within you.

Women that have a habit of showing more appreciation for a man's strengths as opposed to continuously chastising him for his shortcomings tend to make excellent partners in long-term relationships.

She Provides Consistent Support and Encouragement

Both men and women have trust issues in relationships, but for some men, the feelings can be even more intense when it comes to totally trusting a woman for that emotional support they need and want.

Men are naturally more guarded about their emotions than women are. Because of this, we have a more difficult time being completely open with our feelings, inner needs, and conflicts.

Yeah, all the emotional stuff...

One of the reasons for this is because as a man, you need to feel as if you can completely trust a woman with the more tender sides of yourself without thinking that she will perceive you as weak then eventually losing interest in you.

Let's face it; you have your insecurities just like any other human being. And sooner or later the not so pleasant sides of who you are will begin to show themselves. You want to be with a woman that will remain consistent in her support of you regardless of your weaknesses and burdens.

In fact, a good woman is one who will help to heal the emotional scars of your past just as you would with her. Since one of the purposes of a relationship is to lend emotional support and healing, it is important to choose a woman that you harmonize with on all levels.

A man's need to be perceived as the stronger and more powerful of the two genders is deeply ingrained into his psyche. Thus as men, we need to feel as if our woman is completely supportive of us before we can show some of the more intimate sides of ourselves.

A good woman will find unique ways of showing her unwavering support and loyalty. She will grow to become your one-woman cheering squad and your number one source of nurturing over time.

She's a Fountain of Youth and Light-Heartedness

Being a fountain of youth and a source of light-heartedness means that no matter how old a woman gets, she'll still possess a childlike zest for life and be an absolute joy to be around.

Here's a quick tip if you want to find this kind of woman:

Avoid women who appear to be monotonous, dull, and cantankerous.

Let me make this clear…

I cannot stand being around cantankerous women who do nothing but complain and act miserable all the time. I consciously choose not to bitter my soul with the company of such women.

You would be wise to do the same.

One big fear that I used to have when it came to relationships was ending up with a woman who would only grow to become a complete bore, and an utter pain to be around. Knowing that I'd never make it in that kind of relationship, I set out to define exactly what it was that made some women a joy to be around even as they aged.

What I discovered was something simple, and here's what I came up with...

If you want to maintain a fun and fulfilling relationship, choose a woman that has a cheerful, optimistic outlook on life. Find a woman that has a habit of being happy and who chooses to have a sunny disposition.

As men we love adventure, challenge, and excitement. In fact, we need adventure and excitement in our lives just as much as women do, if not more. When a woman is enthusiastic about life itself, and she adds that energy to the relationship, it makes a man even more passionate about her.

Generally speaking, everybody loves being around fun people. No one wants to be around an uninteresting, miserable person for whatever reason.

With this in mind, be on the lookout for the kind of woman that gives off that youthful spark that we all love and adore. And remember, this youthful spark has less to do with how young a woman is, but more to do with how young she *feels* and makes you *feel*.

She may very well become your own fountain of eternal youth, no matter how old you both are.

She Doesn't Allow You to Make Excuses

This one will be difficult for some guys, but I believe it's important to take note of…

If you come across an attractive woman that respects you enough to hold you to your promises and who "keeps you in check" by making sure you stick to your word, you're in the company of an amazing woman.

I know it might be *easier* to settle down with a woman that will only support you and feed your ego, but that's not enough. What we need as men, no, as HIGH-QUALITY men is a woman that's going to stick by our side and ensure that we do the things we said we would do. Whether it's something as simple as running an errand or something grander like pursuing your dreams of being an actor, we need a woman who's not going to *allow* us to lower our standards.

To her, maintaining your integrity as a man should become one of her top priorities in your relationship. And she'll do this by kicking your butt if you're not following through with your word.

Yes, she might "nag" you, but ONLY if you're not being the man that she knows you can be. Trust me on this one. Having a woman by your side that will not only nurture you when you fall down but who will also kick you in the behind when you sit down (due to fear or lack of morals) is a blessing.

A woman that not only recognizes your bad habits but who will firmly hold you to higher ones is a keeper for a man that truly wants to reach his full potential in this world.

The Four Qualities That Make Her a Keeper

There are certain qualities that a man wants in the woman he is interested in romantically. While we all want different qualities in the woman we really desire, there are certain qualities that most men will agree are the basis for what we might call a "good" woman.

But let's face it; no one is perfect.

Not even your "perfect" woman is going to be perfect. However, I'm going to go against conventional wisdom here and say that there IS a woman out there who is PERFECT for YOU. And if you're looking for the kind of woman that is perfect for building a long-term fulfilling relationship with, she's going to have certain qualities that will make her standout from the crowd of women around her.

I'm going to do my best to point out the bulk of these qualities. Of course, this is not a definitive list by any means, but I can guarantee you that a high-quality woman that can make your life much richer and fulfilling will posses most, if not all of these qualities.

1. Confidence

A confident woman is beyond sexy. She's the kind of woman who can be assertive when the time calls for it. She knows what she wants and she's not afraid to stand up for herself and her loved ones. This is definitely the kind of woman you want by your side.

A confident woman will know how to speak her mind in a dignified way without coming across disrespectfully. She trusts her ability to make good decisions that will lead to the best results. You'll find that a confident woman will be quite careful when it comes to choosing a man to place her confidence in as well.

2. Attention to Physical Appearance

This one should be a given. The fact of the matter is, as a man you're driven first by what you see. This is how nature designed you. A smart woman understands this fact, and she will do the best she can to ensure that she remains enticing to your physical senses.

When a woman goes out of her way to make herself appear even more beautiful, then you know that she values her worth. I'm not talking about women who bathe themselves in make-up. I'm simply referring to the kind of women that not only know their intrinsic beauty, but they're quite capable of illustrating that beauty by the way they present and take care of themselves.

For instance, health and fitness are important factors in anyone's life, and a good woman will do what is necessary to ensure that her health is as it should be.

Habitual exercise and proper nutrition are essentials to enjoying good health, and the woman who has a habit of working out and eating right is quite the catch. This is important because it shows that she's committed to maintaining her well-being, and thereby she will make your personal well-being important as well.

Also, a high-quality woman is also aware of how she presents herself in public. She's not trying to be the beauty queen in the way she dresses, but it's important that she knows how to bring out the best of her features.

A woman that can look stunning in a breath-taking outfit and make it all look effortless is worth your time and attention.

3. Competence

One of the most attractive things that a woman can possess is competence. She doesn't have to be a Harvard graduate or even the valedictorian of her class, but she should excel in the area of her interest as well as being able to handle her own responsibilities.

A high-quality woman who is quite efficient at getting things done will definitely stand out. In the long-run, her ability to take care of things when you're not around will become a priceless asset to you.

Trust me on this one.

You will greatly appreciate a woman who can demonstrate good judgment in how she carries out her responsibilities. Even more importantly, it's highly likely that this kind of woman is much more comfortable making tough decisions when dealing with conflict.

I repeat…this is the kind of woman that can become a priceless asset to your future.

4. She Embraces Her Femininity

To me, a high-quality woman embraces that fact that she is, essentially, a woman. This is how nature intended it, and thus a woman should truly embrace it. She never hides her femininity, but instead she realizes that it gives her the confidence to live her life fully.

Maybe it's just me, but I love really feminine women. I love women that know how to naturally demonstrate grace and beauty in their everyday lives.

Think about it. You'll probably find that most women are much more attracted to a man when he takes charge of situations and does things that demonstrate masculine strength and dominance. Even when he dresses in a way that brings out the best of his masculinity you'll find a woman taking more notice.

With this in mind, the same applies for us guys. The more feminine she appears to you, the more naturally attractive she becomes to you.

This is nature's design.

So if you're a sucker for the "princess types" like I am, try to find a woman who embraces her body and wears a style of clothing that brings out her true feminine nature. I love it when a woman wears bright colors and puts on dresses to go out instead of always opting for blue jeans and pants.

Mind you, there's nothing wrong with blue jeans and pants, as they can be quite sexy. But I tend to notice that really feminine women, the ones that I find highly attractive, seem to enjoy skirts and dresses a lot more.

I'm a sucker for a gorgeous woman in a flowing, summer dress. It's the best thing ever!

What Makes Her So Special Anyway?

Okay, so you want to become the kind of man that a good woman simply can't do without. You want to become an irresistible catch that she will respect, admire, and desire and an irreplaceable lover that brings her the kind of happiness and satisfaction that few women ever receive on this earth.

That's excellent, but first, what makes her worth the effort?

I mean, what is it about her that's so special anyway?

What is it that she's bringing to the table to make her worthy of your time and energy?

What makes her so unique among other women that you MUST have a woman like her on your arm?

Lucky for you, I'm here to tell you.

From my own dating experience, successes and failures alike, I've learned that by using three simple words, I can quickly figure out if a woman is worth my attention.

I'm not being snobbish; I'm simply being SELECTIVE. Remember, you're the man, you're the selector, YOU decide what kind of woman you want to attract and build a relationship with, not the other way around.

And it's only with that kind of attitude will you find true happiness and peace of mind in your dating and relationship life.

But I digress...

There are three simple descriptions that will embody what a high-quality, MATURE man thinks of his ideal woman. He will realize that he wants…a woman who is *irresistible*, *indispensable*, and *irreplaceable.*

Even when you consider men who are so called "players", they tend to say the same things about the kind of woman that could make them want to be in a long-term relationship.

Deep down inside all **mature,** high-quality men desire a relationship with a woman that embodies these characteristics in her own special and unique kind of way.

The Irresistible Woman

First, you need to recognize that the kind of woman that will hold your interest will be one that you're deeply attracted to you on all levels. This is the kind of attraction that is mental, physical, and spiritual as well. You must be drawn to her on these levels so that a unique and mind-blowing chemistry can take place between you both.

The irresistible woman has something about her that cannot readily be defined to a man. She leaves him speechless. Her presence commands masculine attention, and her slightest touch can disarm even the most guarded of men.

She will attract you with her natural sexuality and beauty, with her appealing personality, and through her deep connection with your masculine needs and desires.

She will be physically attractive to you, and she will be the kind of woman that appeals to your particular tastes and intellectual interests. This is important if you two are going to be able to talk passionately about anything.

The irresistible woman also displays sexual confidence through her beauty, and how she fully embraces her feminine nature. She is graceful and gracious with others, and thus she possesses a personal magnetism that you simply won't be able to resist.

The Indispensable Woman

Secondly, you'll recognize an indispensable woman because in a relationship she'll grow to become the kind of woman that you can rely on. She'll be the kind of woman who's more likely to be a suitable partner for your particular mission in life.

Since you're a man of high-quality, you will undoubtedly be one that is driven in some capacity by an undeniable passion, mission, or a calling, which means that your ideal mate is a woman who can add value to you on your life's journey.

Of course, you must be able to add value to her life's journey as well, and a good woman will be aware of this, so the more supportive you are of her dreams, passions, and goals, the more she will be willing to support you as well.

The indispensable woman is one who is resourceful and productive in her own daily affairs. This is not to say that she is necessarily perfect in all that she does, but that she shows competence and skill in accomplishing her tasks and achieving her own goals.

In other words, she'll be proactive and not reactive to circumstances and events in her life. She's resourceful and enterprising without the need for outside approval. However, if she does seek approval or support from a man, it's because she chooses to, and because she respects him.

Trust me on this one. You'll be much more attracted now and in the future to a woman who's doing something to strive towards her own goals while living a productive and purposeful life.

This doesn't mean that she'll be trying to change the world or anything, but understand that you'll be much better off with the kind of woman that uses her time and resources wisely.

This is the kind of woman that will be invaluable to you in the long-run.

The Irreplaceable Woman

Thirdly, you need to recognize that your life is and can be much better when you're with her, and that you'd rather not do without.

Often, women have the fear that a man may replace them or leave them for something that they perceive as 'better' or 'newer' somewhere down the line. But this isn't necessarily the case with a relationship based on mutual respect, admiration, and commitment.

If you come across a woman that can maintain her uniqueness, you won't have anything to worry about. And though it is difficult (or impossible) to foretell the future, it is possible to affect it.

The irreplaceable woman is one who is exceptionally different, matchless, and unique to YOU. This doesn't mean that she will have to be or do anything outrageous to stand out in a crowd of women, but there must be something about her that makes her special and rare among her peers.

Undoubtedly, there will be something about you that she'll be attracted to, something that stands out. This maybe something that drives her crazy (in a good way), and she would not change about you.

So in the same way, you should ask yourself, "What makes her so unique that I can't see myself ever giving her up?"

It's usually some quality about her that made you stop and take notice of her. You realize that there's something about her that you know that you need in your life.

Never decide to be with a woman who's just like every other woman out there. What I mean is that she should be comfortable being her authentic self, in the front of you and anyone else.

Though as social creatures we are prone to conformity, the irreplaceable woman does her best to ensure that she's unique. She should desire to not only be herself, but to be the best version of herself as much as possible.

But what will really make her irreplaceable to you is how she harmonizes with your own uniqueness. Just as she would rather not do without you because there's simply no one else like you out there, you should feel the same about her.

This is why it's very important that you become the best version of yourself, and never try to be someone or something that does not harmonize with the core of who you are.

CHAPTER 3:
On Being High-Status And Communicating Value

The Five Qualities That a High-Quality Woman Desires in a Man

It's pretty safe to say that every woman wants something different when it comes to what they find attractive in a man. But from my own observations, research, and personal experience, there are certain universal qualities that high-quality women find highly desirable in a man.

I've decided to list these qualities for you so that you can have an idea of what this kind of woman is looking for. These are the qualities that are the basic characteristics of what we might call a "mature man", which is EXACTLY the kind of man that a worthwhile woman is looking for.

1. Self-Confidence

Self-confidence is basically a feeling of trust in your abilities, qualities, and judgment in any given situation. The most desired quality to have as a man is courage, and self-confidence is one of the ways in which you communicate to the world your level of courage.

But we often hear a lot of talk about guys having self-confidence, but how do we properly define it in a situation?

Here's an example…

Let's say for instance that you're kind of hopeless when it comes to playing basketball, but you can still remain confident in your demeanor, simply because you don't place a great deal of emphasis on the outcome of your performance.

The key element to self-confidence is, therefore, an acceptance of the countless consequences of a particular situation, whether they are good or bad. When you refuse to dwell on negative consequences, you can be more self-confident because you're not worrying about failure or (more accurately) the disapproval of others following potential failure.

With this kind of mental attitude, you are more likely to focus on the actual situation, which means that enjoyment, and success in that situation is also more probable.

The opposite of self-confidence is insecurity, and it's like a disease; a disease that no woman wants to get infected with.

Think of self-confidence as the act of <u>confiding in yourself</u>. In other words, it's as if you're putting trust in yourself to do your best in any given situation, no matter what the outcome may be.

The self-confident man possesses an inner calm and an outer poise that shows in his actions. He is all right with himself and the world around him, and he can get the most out of any moment because he's learned to control his imagination, and thereby controls his emotional state.

2. Self-Control

The amount of self-control you possess will lie in your ability to control your emotions and desires, or the expression of them in your behavior, especially in difficult situations. In other words, your level of self-control tends to show itself a lot more when you have to make decisions in the midst of conflict.

This characteristic is extremely attractive to a woman simply because a self-controlled man is one she can't walk over, control, or manipulate. And yes, the mere fact a woman won't be able to do that to you makes her want you even more.

Strange isn't it?

Remaining poised and in control of your emotions in a difficult situation assures a woman of your ability to handle the stresses of life. It illustrates your strength of mind and your resiliency since you won't be easily swayed by outside events and circumstances.

It shows that you can lead yourself, and therefore you have the potential to lead others.

Sometimes self-control is used interchangeably with self-discipline. But whereas self-discipline may refer to the training that one gives oneself to accomplish a certain task or to adopt a particular pattern of behavior, even if one would rather be doing something else, self-control is how you apply this disciplined behavior in real life situations.

For example, denying oneself an extravagant pleasure in order to accomplish a more demanding charitable deed is a display of self-discipline.

Thus, self-discipline is the assertion of willpower over more base desires. And virtuous behavior results when your motivations are aligned with your reasoned aims, which is to do what you know is best and to do it gladly. A good woman, the kind that can and will bring more happiness and success into your life greatly appreciates a man of virtue.

You can develop greater self-control by learning to take conscious control of your own emotional states. By becoming more aware of your thoughts, words, and actions you can learn to become the master of your moods and your emotions. This will help you to handle rapid changes in the outside world that take you out of your comfort zone.

Your responses to the things happening around you won't be based on fear, but they'll be based on a deeper knowledge of your ability to handle anything. What women love about a man with self-control and self-discipline is that she knows that she can count on him at any time to make the best decision.

3. Ambition

If you were to ask any attractive and successful woman who knew what she wanted out of life what qualities she wanted in her ideal mate, one of the top answers would be ambition. These women instinctively know that a man can have all sorts of wonderful qualities that can make for a great relationship, but if he lacks ambition, she knows that he won't hold her interest for very long.

Ambition is attractive to high-quality women because it communicates that you possess goals, dreams, plans, or some sort of vision for your life that you're working on bringing about in the future.

It is the desire for personal achievement, and using that desire to assert yourself in the world to get what you want. Ambition provides the motivation and determination necessary to achieve goals in life. Ambitious people seek to be the best at what they choose to do for attainment, power, or superiority.

And here's something I want you to keep in mind:

When a man has an insatiable passion for achieving a worthwhile goal, he becomes much more desirable to the women he wants.

If you've ever wondered why many extremely desirable, quality women end up with guys who may not display the outward signs of what we think is success, just keep in mind that they probably display the inward signs of great success.

A good woman can notice this with unusual ease.

Thus, it's important to have some kind of ambition and to be working towards some worthwhile goal. This is especially important when trying to find the RIGHT woman for you because she must be willing to share or invest her time and energy in your ambitions.

Only by choosing a woman that is willing to support you (as you support her as well), can you attain durable fulfillment in your life and your relationship.

4. Stimulating Personality

A good woman loves a man who knows how to have fun, how to be friendly, and how to make her laugh. I could have just mentioned that women love a guy who knows a few good jokes since humor is VERY important, but it goes a bit beyond that.

And no, stimulating a woman is not about putting on a show for her or being her personal clown. It's more about engaging her senses through lingual and non-lingual communication.

To be stimulating is to be fun and friendly. It's about being warm and engaging in conversation, to be amusing when you need to be, and at times persuasive. It's all about being interesting enough so that she's not bored with you in seconds. In fact, to be really stimulating is to have her begging for more of your attention.

If you can do this my friend, you're in a very, very happy place.

Women love to feel stimulated. It's no different for humans than it is for other creatures in the animal kingdom. Just watch one of those wildlife documentaries and you'll see what I mean.

The males of the species are always doing something to arouse interest in the female. They're always doing something to "stimulate" the female's interest in order to create a mating opportunity. Showing off an array of feathers, fighting another rival male in front of the herd, or even building an elaborate home complete with threads and colorful garbage (I watch a lot of wildlife documentaries), it's all to engage the female's curiosities.

And yes, we men do the exact same thing.

But the stimulating man is more than just "funny"; he's interesting and friendly as well. He's somehow managed to fuse together the right amount of charm, wit, and body language that communicates to women that he's a fun and friendly guy who's a blast to be around.

Don't get me wrong here, you don't have to be the life of the party, but you must be interesting *to her*. Be interesting and engaging in SOMETHING. Trust me, there are enough women out there with enough interests that you'll find someone who's just as fascinated as you are about whatever it is you're fascinated with.

And sometimes it's not what you're fascinated with that matters, it's all about how you communicate it to others.

5. Unique Abilities or Passionate Interests

Women love it when a man has something in his life that he is either extremely passionate about or incredibly skilled at. Either one will do, as a high-quality woman usually comes with her own set of skills, abilities, and interests that she'll want to share and develop with her ideal man.

Be passionate about something, or be obsessive with some particular skill or talent you have. It should be something that is unique to you, something in which you have an enormous amount of untapped potential.

If you have a talent for painting for instance, and historical paintings are something you're extremely passionate about, your ideal woman will be able to share in that passion with you. In fact, it'll probably be one of the things she finds incredibly sexy about you.

If you're a business owner and your particular industry is something that you're incredibly passionate about, the right woman for you will be able to share in that passion and your enthusiasm might be the very thing that draws her into your world.

So you should consider seeking to develop some particular talent of yours, since high-quality women love a man with some sort of unique genius. Or you can become quite learned and passionate about something that has the potential to make you stand out from the crowd, since your ideal woman will be someone who can share and potentially invest herself in your particular interests.

Why Most Guys Fail With Remarkable Women

A lot of guys often wonder why it is that certain women just seem to totally ignore them. They find themselves at a loss when it comes to attracting really high-quality women. They simply do not have a clue how to go about getting one of these exceptionally amazing women to go out with them or to even get their attention.

For starters, these gorgeous and intelligent women are for the most part attainable for any guy who is willing to step his game up. But the fact of the matter is that these guys are simply invisible to these kinds of women, and here are the main reasons why...

Most Guys Are Simply Uninteresting

To a high-quality woman who has a TON of options when it comes to dating men, most guys are simple carbon copies of every other guy she's met. In other words they are BORING. Only remarkable products get bought on the market from big spenders, just like how remarkable people are noticed by those just like them. Like attracts like.

This is simple social science.

If you want to attract a remarkable woman, then learn to become a remarkable kind of guy. Find ways to stand out in a crowd. Develop a style of your own, a way of speaking, a way of dressing, and a way of acting. It's better to be different and misunderstood than to be accepted in a crowd of other boring people.

Make your life something remarkable. Do you have any interesting hobbies or past times? What about your friends? Are they interesting or just as boring as you are?

Find ways to become a much more interesting and remarkable person by going to work on yourself. Make your life and your personality highly attractive and interesting and you'll have no problems getting the attention of highly attractive and interesting women.

I just want to add here that you shouldn't make an attempt to be something you're not. But do keep in mind that 'YOU' are a fluid concept. So long as you're not trying to imitate someone else, 'YOU' are whatever you DECIDE to be.

So if you decide to become a more interesting, remarkable person because you're attracted to more interesting and remarkable women, then go for it. If you really want to change yourself to improve your results in life, don't let anyone tell you otherwise.

Remember, who YOU are is a fluid concept that can be improved upon so that you're more in alignment with what it is you want to attract into your life. Choosing to evolve consciously as a man is never a bad idea.

Most Guys Worship Very Beautiful, High-Quality Women

A lot of guys grow up with the idea that really gorgeous women want you to shower them with gifts and compliments and treat them like beauty queens. I should know, because I was one of these poor fools. In fact, the truth is quite the opposite.

This goes along with the first reason why extremely gorgeous women ignore most men. Most men that are interested in them are boring, and to add to this, these kinds of women are just as bored with the way men treat them as well. These kinds of women are simply not being challenged enough.

I think the phrase that "girls just want to have fun" rings true here. Gorgeous, highly attractive women just want to have as much fun as the next girl, maybe even more.

The problem is that most guys treat them with such awe and adoration that they fail to do anything to challenge them and have fun with them. If a beautiful and intelligent woman has grown up this way most of her life, then she's probably only met a handful of men that have consistently challenged her and given her a sense of fun and excitement.

If you want to attract and keep a total-package woman, then stop worshiping her and putting her on a pedestal. She's a human being just like anyone else, and deep down inside she knows it.

When you come across a high-quality woman, treat her with respect, but treat her just like another human being.

The more you can relate to these kinds of women on an *authentic* level of equality and remind them in charming and humorous ways that there isn't anything too spectacular about them, the more they will appreciate and take notice of you.

You're not being a mean jerk; you're simply being upfront and truthful.

Do this in a fun way and communicate that you are comfortable with her beauty, and that you're more concerned about her personality and character.

Read that last sentence again.

A woman who's ALWAYS being approached and hit on by men has probably seen and heard it all. So if you really want to impress her, adopt the attitude that you're trying to assess the quality of her character.

Think of yourself as the one who is choosing her rather than the other way around.

Oh, and please write this down someplace where you can see it every day:

Do NOT tolerate any disrespectful behavior from her or anyone else for that matter, and for heaven's sake do NOT be a predictable wuss of a man by always giving her exactly what she wants.

If you don't want to be the guy that gets ignored by really gorgeous and intelligent women, then learn to stand up for yourself and to stand out from the crowd.

Become a remarkable guy and begin enjoying your life. Work on yourself and associate with remarkable people who also lead interesting lives as well.

As you begin to become a more highly attractive and high-quality guy in terms of having an interesting personality, lifestyle, and useful skills, you'll attract more high-quality women into your life as well. Just remember to treat really gorgeous women like you would an old buddy. In other words, don't worship her or put her on a pedestal.

Remember, gorgeous women are genuinely bored with the average guy and his adoration for her. Challenge her, tease her, and just learn to have fun with her, no matter how 'out of your league' you think she may be.

Do this and she'll simply be swept off her feet by her interactions with you, and will want to be around you more and more. Why? Because you'll be giving her the 'one thing' that few men ever illustrate to her on any given day.

What is this 'one thing' that few men ever give her. One word…

Authenticity.

So remember, don't worship her. Treat her like a human being and have some fun with her. The more she realizes that you're not impressed by how pretty she is, the more she'll be impressed by your confidence and sincerity.

How to Be Authentically Attractive

I'm sure you've heard people tell you over and over again that the most important thing for you to do in order to attract and keep the RIGHT woman who is ideal for you is to be yourself. Well, they're only half right.

What do I think about this? Well, I think you should definitely be yourself, but don't stop there. You should try to be the best version of yourself. What I mean is that you should focus on you. Focus on becoming the kind of man that can attract and maintain a healthy, long-term, and fulfilling romantic relationship with a high-quality woman.

And believe it or not, you can best accomplish this by not only being the most authentic version of yourself, but by being the best version of that self as well.

In fact, you should always aim to be the most mature and manly version of that self. Here are a few ideas to help you navigate through your dating experiences with women.

Be Mysterious

Here's the cold hard truth. A woman wants to get to know the REAL you, but she doesn't want it all at once. She doesn't need to know every last detail about your life straight out the gate. You don't need to advertise your achievements or tell her about your massive collection of transformer action figures as soon as you meet her.

Give her some time to become a bit more attached to you before you start revealing every single part of your life to her. She'll enjoy the mystery of it all.

Trust me.

The more mysterious and laid back you are the more rare and attractive you will appear to her. Really, think about it.

Nobody wants what's considered common. We're all after something unique in our lives and the same applies to a woman.

Even if you've already attracted the woman of your dreams, she'll probably enjoy it a bit more if you can continuously surprise her and add a bit more mystery and adventure to your relationship.

A little (or a lot) of ambiguity combined with romance can drive a woman crazy, the good kind of crazy. Why? Well, because she'll spend most of her time trying to figure you out. And the more time she spends thinking about you, the more she'll become interested in you.

You see where this is going right?

If you're just meeting her and she wants to know more about you, try to divert her questions and tell her you'll answer her later once you think you can trust her. Have fun with her!

Or even better, you can be extremely vague with your responses. For example, if you work in a hotel and she asks what you do for a living, tell her that you're in the business of leisure and luxury. And say it with a smirk on your face.

I know, it sounds crazy. But always remember:

Girls just want to have fun!

Nothing can be more fun for her than trying to figure out this interesting, yet mysterious guy who's quite fun and though he's giving her such a hard time.

A quality woman will appreciate the challenge.

Tease Her Playfully

If you're going to be more attractive to the woman you want, then you might have to learn to be a bit challenging. Believe me, women want just as much of a challenge as men do. They want to feel the excitement of getting to know someone new and interacting with an interesting stranger. And one of the best ways to do this is to…tease her.

If you can combine a bit of humor with a shot of confidence, you've got what it takes to tease a woman so she'll never forget you. Just so we're clear though, teasing her has nothing to do with being a cocky bastard. Of course, cocky bastards do tend to attract women, but not the kind of woman you're after.

A high-quality woman won't stand long for verbal abuse or jerk-like behavior for long if at all. She has WAY more class and intelligence than that.

Teasing a woman is considered the same thing as flirting with her. It embodies the attitude of, "I think I'm a pretty great guy, so you should too", but in a playful way.

Making outrageous demands and giving ridiculous responses to her questions will not only help to build the sexual tension between you two, but it will also make her laugh as long as you can be humorous in your interaction.

Laughter is perhaps the greatest communication tool for making someone else comfortable with you. It puts them in a state of joy and bliss and we can become quite addicted to someone's personality because of their ability to put a smile on our faces.

Mix a bit of that very same humor with an outlandish yet confident request and you'll watch her light up right before you.

For example, let's say that you're at a party of some other chic social environment and you've been talking to her for a while. Saying something like, "Okay, so I've been chatting with you for quite some time now and you haven't even offered to get me a drink. I'm

61

beginning to think you're not the lady I thought you were."

I know, it's a bit out there, but a fun, confident woman will "get the hint" that you're flirting and she'll gladly take the bait.

Other things such as making light fun of her for doing something embarrassing will create massive levels of attraction in a woman. It's as if you're treating her like a little sister who's misbehaving. It's not about annoying her, but rather it's about being a fun and entertaining nuisance. It takes guts, but that's what she's LOOKING FOR.

Blaming her for something silly is also a great way to spark her attraction. When she interacts with you, twist her words around playfully to make it seem like she said something ridiculous, and then get on her case for it. Give her a hard, but outrageously playful time.

For instance, if I ask her what did she study in college and she tells me that she studied marine biology; I'll proceed to look her dead in the eye with an amused look on my face and say, "So…you have a degree in water animals? Are you serious? Why would anyone get a degree in water animals, dude?" And then I proceed to laugh at her.

Yeah, you had to have been there, but I'm telling you, this WORKED like a charm. She was laughing at herself as well and began to defend herself, thereby getting deeper into conversation and more comfortable with me.

Don't worry, not every woman will engage you, but that's not the point. You're looking for the kind of woman who is comfortable dealing with men and confident enough to be laid back and playful.

Another kind of playful teasing is playful banter. It's kind of like a back and forth between two people who just seem to "get it". They have chemistry together and the teasing is being bounced off of each other.

This is when a woman really gets it. You say something flirty to tease her and she says something flirty to tease you right back. Or you both engage in a kind of mind game where you're trying to outsmart one another with witty dialogue.

It's quite fun. And if you're anything like me you'll use this one a lot, since a really intelligent woman will LOVE it when you can playfully captivate her mind with stimulating yet nonsensical conversation.

Be Honest and Direct

You didn't see this one coming did you? That's fine, because most guys don't realize that a high-quality woman finds an honest man HIGHLY attractive. It displays your character to her and it reassures her of just how much you stand out from other men.

But what do I mean by honesty? I mean don't hold your punches. If there's something that a woman does that does not line up with your highest ideals, be firm and point out that you don't agree with it.

I'm not saying to go about pointing out all the things you're not satisfied with, I simply mean that if an opportunity arises for you to be completely honest with her, take it. Most men will take the easy way out and either lie or find a way to avoid conflict. But you're not like most men, and you don't want to be like most men do you?

Take the tough road and be honest. Have firm opinions on things and don't be afraid to share them. If you're going to be your authentic self, the best version of your authentic self, then you must be honest with yourself first and foremost and with her.

You can still be fun, playful, and mysterious while being honest. In fact, if you can incorporate a bit of directness in your flirting, it'll be twice as potent. For instance, if you really want to compliment her appearance or something that stands out about her, be honest and direct with it and tell her what you think. If she has some enormous earrings, tell her that you think her earrings are kind of huge, but also point out that they help to bring out her tantalizing smile.

Be direct, but say it playfully.

A comment like that will catch her off guard. You're pointing out your opinion on her choice of earrings, but you're making a connection by complimenting something else about her.

It works.

But just so you'll know when to be completely upfront and when to be flirty, vague, or mysterious, here's a tip:

When she asks you for your opinion on something she's serious about, be honest and truthful. Don't sugar coat anything. If she does something you're not too particularly pleased with, be honest about it. If someone around you is acting in a way that insults your very soul, be honest and upfront about it and refuse to support that kind of behavior. A quality woman will find this HIGHLY attractive.

The best thing you can do when first getting to know a woman is to initiate what I like to call, "The Honesty Code." Tell her that you think she's interesting, but that you're only going to continue to hang out with her under ONE condition. The condition is that she must be completely honest and upfront with you about everything. Tell her that she must be authentic, real, and her natural self and that you'll appreciate it if she expects the same from you.

Listen, if you can do this ONE thing with a high-quality woman, she will IMMEDIATELY place you in a separate category from other men she's dated and she will become VERY interested in getting to know you more intimately.

Trust me on this one. Women are doing everything they can to find an honest, bold, and upfront guy who they can trust and respect. Be that guy.

Use the Art of Detachment

If you want to be the kind of guy that a high-quality woman finds irresistible then you're going to have to learn the art of detachment. As long as you act as if it doesn't matter if you fail or not, you won't fail because you'll be having way too much fun.

Being detached in this context has several meanings.

Firstly, you must learn to give a woman her space when you're interacting with her. As you two get to know one another and become more intimate later on, there'll be plenty of time for being all up and under each other as a couple. But for right now, give her some space.

What this will communicate to her is that you're not a needy guy who's desperately looking for a woman. Women can smell desperation from a mile away, and they immediately run in the opposite direction.

Secondly, as you interact with her, just seem as if you're uninterested in trying to get something out the situation. Have a confident, winning attitude that communicates that you know you're a great guy, and you don't need to prove it to anyone. Be laid back and friendly, and act as if nothing else matters but the moment.

This is what people really mean when they say someone is cool. They're detached from it all. They're not too invested in the outcomes, but rather they're just enjoying the moment and ensuring that everyone is having a good time.

You're not thinking about if she'll want to see you again or if you're going to say something stupid. You simply don't care.

You're not thinking if you should call first or if she'll call you. Why? Well, because you simply don't care about the outcome.

The more detached you are from a situation the more clearly you can think and the more engaged you'd be in the moment. Spending too much time thinking about future results is the surest way to failure in any area of life. Just focus on the moment and feel confident that things will always work out.

In fact, adopt this attitude, or better yet use it as a self-talk whenever you feel as if you're trying too hard or that you might fail:

"It doesn't matter if she likes me or not. I like me a lot, and that's all that matters. I like myself because I respect myself, and people like me because they respect me. Besides, I think I'm a pretty cool person and I only want to know if she's a pretty cool person as well. If she doesn't end up liking me, that's fine. And if she does end up liking me, that's fine as well. Not being liked has never killed anyone. So whatever happens, I'm OKAY with it, and it really doesn't matter to me either way because I'm definitely going to have a good time no matter what."

Commit to having as much fun as humanly possible in any social situation and you'll have uncovered an untapped source of serendipitous power. Oh, and I suggest that you write that little self-talk on a big sheet of paper and stick it up somewhere you can read it every day. Or better yet, write that on a card and keep it in your pocket or in your wallet and carry it around with you. Read it right before you interact with any woman and use it as your "Coolness Credo".

Let it be your philosophy when it comes to interacting not just with women, but also with anyone in general. It's a great way to look at the world, since you'll never need the approval of others to make you feel a sense of worth and value.

Believe me, if you read this book and this is the only technique that you master, you'll be much happier in life when it comes to your relationships. And a good woman will appreciate you more simply because you don't let things get to you, even her.

When a woman realizes that she isn't the deciding factor in your peace of mind, she'll become ridiculously interested and attracted to you. She'll want to know what makes you tick, what your thoughts are, and how you live your life. By being detached, you essentially end up succeeding simply because you didn't really care too much about it.

It's like you see success as inevitable to you. Because you believe it, it will be. And the less you worry about success, the easier it will be for you.

It's a paradox, but one that works. So use it.

Become the Superior Choice to the Woman You Want

A woman we might consider to be the "Total Package" is not the kind of woman who's interested in wasting her time when it comes to men. This is why it's important for you to communicate your high value to her early on and continuously as you interact with her.

Women like this come across men who want their time and attention very often, thus they can be extremely selective. They're quite used to having guys chase after them in order to get their approval, and quite frankly, they're tired of it.

What she actually wants is a fun challenge. She doesn't want to be with a guy who's easy to please. She wants a man that has firm personal boundaries, refined tastes, and high standards for himself.

Simply put, she wants a man who knows what he wants and who's determined to have it. She'll eventually lose interest or never have an interest in a man who doesn't have high but reasonable standards.

But why is this so? Well, a good woman wants and needs a man she respects and admires so that she can work on making him happy. She wants someone that she has to go out of her way for, not because she has to, but because she wants to.

But if you're the kind of guy that's pretty much happy with whatever she has to offer, she'll feel cheapened. She'll think that you can be satisfied with any woman that comes along, and that's not a comforting feeling for her.

If a woman can land a guy with high standards, she'll feel as if she's won the lottery. She'll be proud to be with a high-quality man because she knows that he doesn't just settle for anything and anyone. She'll feel that you're a catch and that she caught you and this is a very important feeling for her to have.

What's even more important is that she'll feel fulfilled and happy knowing that you chose her out of every other woman based not just on her beauty, but her uniqueness and her virtue. She'll feel that she earned your affection and that she's irreplaceable to you. It's that feeling of her being your one and only woman that gives her a deep sense of security and accomplishment as a worthwhile woman.

What she also wants is a man who is so confident in himself that he could really care less whether she approves of him or not. In fact, she craves to be with an honest, confident, loving, and ambitious man who can make her feel desirable while making himself desirable to her as well. She wants the opportunity to yearn for a man worthy of her, but the guys she comes across on a daily basis simply cannot give her that opportunity.

Truly, what she wants is a guy that can keep up with her. She's so tired of men catering to her every wish and desire in order to get her approval that she simply does not even notice them anymore. In her mind, she's DESPERATELY looking and waiting for some guy to come along who is on her level or higher in terms of personal value.

And believe me, the more you work on yourself to develop the kind of character and personality that is the best version of your unique self, the better your chances will be in attracting the ideal high-quality woman of your dreams.

Enhancing Your Personal Value

Your personal value is simply your own self-estimation. Whatever you believe about yourself in terms of what you have to offer the world is your sense of personal value. This makes up your self-image and the more powerful and capable your self-image is the more powerful and capable your personal value to yourself and others will be.

A beautiful woman who has her act together has a better self-image than most other women. She has a better idea of who she is and what she's capable of, and she's only interested in men that can continuously bring out the best in her because they know how to bring out the best in themselves. But this is where you can easily separate yourself from every other guy out there.

How? By consciously pursuing some form of self-development.

I know, you're probably scratching your head at this point, but let me explain this mind-blowing idea.

What is it that every woman wants to do to a man?

Get your mind out of the gutter; I'm being serious here.

You give up? Every woman in some form or fashion wants to either change a man to suit her needs, which is bad, or she wants to influence him to become the best version of himself, which is good.

A good woman will belong to the latter category. This is why your conscious pursuit of self-development WILL make you stand out from any other guy out there.

Because a good woman wants to be a positive influence on a man, she's actually looking for a man with a high potential for PERSONAL GROWTH.

Please stop for a moment and let that sink in.

A good woman with a lot to offer a man doesn't want to be with a guy who's looking to settle in life. She doesn't want anything to do with a man that wastes his time and energy doing nothing worthwhile because he'll do the same with her. She will literally RUN from a man who isn't engaged in some form of learning or personal development activity.

Why? Because what she's really looking for is a man who has the habit of improving himself consistently. She realizes that any man who is actively seeking new ways to improve himself expects the best from himself and that he'll also expect the best from her as well.

I hope that bit of wisdom takes a load off of your back in thinking that you had to become the "perfect man" in order to get the woman of your dreams.

Like I said before, no one's perfect. BUT, her perfect man is the one that is ideal for HER and he's the kind of guy who's always striving for the next level of growth in his own life.

He's the kind of guy who's constantly evolving in all areas of his life, and he's doing so off of his own volition.

What this communicates to a woman is that you're more than willing to better yourself and to reach your highest potential while you're here on this earth. I cannot begin to tell you how attractive this is to a good woman.

When she comes across this one of a kind guy who has a passion for self-development in all areas of his life, she'll become quite interested in him. This is why it's so important for you to follow your own path and stay on it, because the woman that can enhance your life and make you much more happy and successful will be attracted to your passion, your focus, and your drive to <u>grow</u> and excel.

This easily separates you from most guys out there because they're simply not interested in pursuing some form of conscious self-development. Heck, most guys aren't even really that interested in some form of worthwhile achievement.

This is good news for you my friend.

How to Communicate Your Value

Learning new skills and getting good at something will build your overall self-confidence. By taking up fun and interesting hobbies, you're actually bringing a new dimension to your life and allowing yourself to explore your own potentialities. All of this helps to build a powerful self-image as being a capable and productive man, and this is something that you cannot hide from a good woman.

There are many ways you can communicate your high value and your uniqueness to the woman you're with. For example, are you an excellent cook, a master of the kitchen? If you are, then cook for her. Instead of going to some restaurant be creative and plan a delicious meal for her and let her taste your skills.

This is just an example of how easy it is to incorporate your passion into your dating life. What you want is for the woman you're with to see you in your element. We all know that first impressions are lasting impressions, so start things off by showing her some of the areas that you excel in effortlessly.

Whatever you're great at, good at, or getting good at, let her see it. Somehow, get her to interact with you and let your true budding genius shine. Even a more cerebral habit like reading for instance can be put on display by showing her your vast collection of books or by suggesting to her a bookstore shopping date.

You can even use your vast storehouse of knowledge to impress her and teach her something new. And since you're obviously only interested in attracting a great woman who's right for you, you won't have to worry about looking like a complete nerd in front of her.

If she's the right woman, the things that interest you and make you a better and more interesting man will interest her and make you attractive to her as well.

This is why having hobbies that increase your manly skills is so essential. It helps you to become the best version of your natural self, and so it's much easier to attract the right kind of woman.

Your hobbies and path of personal growth makes you seem dynamic, attractive, and very interesting to the woman of your dreams. It displays your creativity, your ingenuity, and your desire to try new things and maximize all of your latent talents and abilities. All this tells her that you're the kind of man that loves to learn new things, and that's a quality that she can support one-hundred percent.

Remember, if there's one thing that she simply cannot stand in a relationship, it's boredom.

Choosing Your Hobbies

A love for lifelong learning is the lifeblood of a healthy lifestyle for the mature man. Mastering a skill or partaking in a passionate interest will make a man extremely attractive to the right woman.

Keep in mind though that the hobbies themselves won't attract your ideal woman, but your passion for them and improving yourself will. You simply cannot hide passion, so ensure that you choose something that makes you feel alive just thinking about it.

Doing something besides watching mindless television will keep your mind well honed and sharp as a man. You'll have an advantage over your peers and your specialized knowledge and experiences will make you stand out.

Just remember to have fun with your hobbies and keep searching for something that engages you totally. Choose hobbies that make you forget about the other stresses in your life and make you feel as if time is flying by when you're doing it.

The more fun it is for you, the more attractive it will make you to the woman of your dreams.

Use the Internet and look for something that grabs your interest and give it a go. Just remember to have fun with it as it should be something that makes time fly whenever you're engaged in it.

CHAPTER 4:
Setting The Foundations For
A Long-Term Relationship

The Paradox of Attracting Romantic Relationships

There's a paradox that exists when it comes to women and dating. It's all about how guys who DON'T necessarily WANT a relationship sometimes end up attracting great women who want nothing more than to be with them indefinitely.

I've noticed this interesting paradox over the course of my dating life and watching my friends with their dating habits. It was a strange phenomenon to watch.

The more a guy (myself included) wanted a loving, committed relationship with a wonderful woman, the less potential mates I would meet. But whenever I simply got into the "groove" of living my life, enjoying myself, and working on personal development, opportunities for relationship bliss with lovely women just seemed to pop up out of nowhere.

It's a strange phenomenon, and it's something that works not only in your dating life, but in other areas of your life as well.

You may realize this yourself with some other area of your life. Sometimes the more relaxed you are about trying to accomplish something, the easier it is for you to bring it into reality.

I'm not talking about being lazy here, because putting in the work to attain anything worthwhile IS a necessity. But what I want you to think about is how your attitude plays a part in all of this.

Attitude is Everything

When it comes to dating and relating to women, your attitude is everything. Guys who project an attitude of confidence and independence are highly attractive to women because this signals that they're not *needy*.

If you project an attitude of neediness and anxiousness to be in a relationship, you'll scare quality women away because of your inner desire to "fill some hole" in your life with her. You're coming from a scarcity mindset, and whether you've just met her or have been out with a woman a few times, she'll soon catch wind of your neediness and she'll be out of your life faster than you can say, "I can't believe I'm going to die alone!"

Make no mistake; being anxious about anything will impede its attainment.

Whether it's a great romantic relationship with a gorgeous young lady or that promotion that you want to land at work; an anxious and needy attitude can and will repel the things you want the most.

A Word on Confidence

A lot of guys think that confidence is everything. Well, confidence does play a major role in both getting a girlfriend AND keeping her happy. But confidence is simply a part of the bigger picture.

That bigger picture, as I've said before, is your attitude.

You see, as I've already mentioned, a woman, the kind of woman that you really want to be in a relationship with, wants to think that she's *worthy* of being in a relationship with you. After she's figured out that you're *worthy* of her attention she actually wants to experience the challenge of catching you and keeping you all to herself.

A smart man knows how to show just enough interest to spark a woman's interest in him, but he knows when to give her enough space so that she has to do a bit of work to sustain his attention as well.

Now, I don't believe in playing mind games with a woman, but I do believe in the power of attraction. If you want to attract a great girlfriend you're going to have to learn how to keep her interested in pursuing you. And the best way to achieve this is by projecting a detached attitude towards romantic relationships, at first at least.

I know, it doesn't make sense, but that's the paradox. The more detached you are from something, the more opportunities for its attainment seem to occur.

If You Build it...She'll Come

Let me keep this as simple as I possibly can…

If you work on becoming what women call "perfect boyfriend material" you'll soon find yourself in situations that actually make having a girlfriend who's enormously invested in you, an absolute guarantee.

You see, this takes all of the pressure off of you. You don't have to worry about impressing a woman to make her want you. Even if you're already dating a woman, you don't have to work so hard just to make her happy.

When you focus on becoming better boyfriend material, a good woman will do whatever she can to ensure that your eyes stay fixed on her. I can promise you that.

This is the beginning of relationship management, because it takes two people to start a relationship. If you give a woman all you've got right out of the gate, there's a high chance that she'll lose interest in you because she'll feel as if she doesn't have to work for your love and affection.

Trust me on this; she wants to feel as if she's *earned* your attention and affection in the long-run. This is how enjoyable relationships begin, because we as human beings will take for granted that which we did not work for.

Relationships are give and take; they are not just give OR take. So if your goal is to get a great girlfriend, you need to keep her interested in you by giving her the gift of chasing you just as much as you chase her. Trust me, she'll love you for it in the end.

The Caged Bird Philosophy: How to Make Her Want You All to Herself

Your ideal woman wants to put you in a cage.

Yes, a cage.

She wants to come across a man that is so enticing, so wonderful, and so right for HER, that she'll do whatever she possibly can to get him in a relationship with her. But don't worry; if you want a great girlfriend like her this is a good thing.

To her, a good catch is like a rare songbird that she would love to have all to herself every single day. Half the fun for her is getting that songbird into her own special cage that she's built for him.

You my friend are that rare songbird.

Or are you?

Here's the caged bird philosophy in a nutshell:

You should really be as free as a bird. You should be enjoying your life, singing, and happy as a wild bird can possibly be. Your ideal woman wants a bird like you, and she wants to trap a bird like you in a cage of commitment.

However, if a wild bird like you flew freely into her cage, seeking asylum, she'll begin to think that something might be wrong with this "wild" bird. She really doesn't want a bird that's going out of his way to be in a cage. <u>*That's no fun.*</u> *She wants a bird that is free, wild, fun-loving, and happy with his life.*

In other words, she wants a good catch, and a good catch will not fly into a cage of commitment as if his life depended on it.

Although your mission is to become the perfect guy and sweep her off of her feet, this does not mean that you're supposed to just commit to her from the get go without her trying to entice you as well.

Think about it.

When a woman says that she wants to be swept off of her feet, she means that she'd rather not see it coming. And when a woman says that she's looking for that perfect guy who's a great catch, she really, really wants to CATCH him.

How are you going to sweep her off of her feet if she can smell your neediness from a mile away? How are you going to be her perfect catch if you're throwing yourself at her?

No.

Don't even think about it.

Romance and seduction begin with the mindset that you are a high-quality guy, and that your time and attention are important. You must have the mindset that you're just as important as anyone else, and that no woman is above or better than you.

Think of yourself as a perfect catch. See yourself as that enticing yet elusive guy that she (and other high-quality women) want to get to know intimately simply because you are worth her time and attention.

Never give any woman, no matter how wonderful and perfect she may appear, all of you straight out of the gate.

Of course, I'm not saying that you shouldn't be honest, but make it fun, and make her chase you just a little. If you give her too much attention too early in the game, you're only going to come off as needy and common.

And no high-quality woman wants common.

In all honesty, the only time completely giving of yourself to a woman will be beneficial to you is after she is already in love with you.

Do keep that in mind.

Your job is to act the part, and make it clear that you're the selector. While you may entertain a woman's company, you're only going to become intimate with her if you're sure that she is right for you.

A strong and confident man has an air about him that communicates that he is cautious and calculating in the kinds of women that he spends his time with, and that he doesn't need to obsess over one woman.

Your success will be based on how well you communicate the fact that you are a good catch for your ideal woman. Ensure that you make it clear through your words and body language that you're interested in seeing if she meets your standards (if she's fun, cheerful, interesting, smart, etc.). Do this by being laid back with her, mysterious, good-humored, and of course…confident.

Make Her Chase You For a Relationship

In all honesty, this concept may blow your mind a bit, but it is guaranteed to skyrocket your success with high-quality women when it comes to starting a healthy long-term relationship. You MUST stand by this one principle. If you do, your life will be a heck of a lot easier.

When you first meet a woman, it is IMPERATIVE that she has the potential for being in a relationship with you. You MUST set your standards high and know what you want first of all, and then you mustn't allow any woman to deter you from those guidelines. Do not even entertain women longer than you have to as soon as you realize that they lack something that is extremely important to you.

Develop the manly habit of being willing to *walk away* from any situation that doesn't work for you. Walk away. Don't entertain her; just walk away.

For example, if you don't date women who smoke, don't make an exception because she's drop dead gorgeous. You're not being authentic with yourself or her.

If you don't date women who use foul language, be willing to let her know that things between you both aren't going to work. The same applies if your guidelines state that you don't date women who flake out on you. Be willing to walk away my friend. It will make you far more attractive to high-quality women and it will also give you an air of supreme confidence that only few men seem to possess in this world.

You cannot "build" a relationship with conversation, gifts, and exciting dates. No. That's merely cultivation. It's like having a garden. You want to spend most of your time cultivating the plants and ensuring that they're growing and bearing fruit. It's not like farming where you'd spend a majority of your time tilling the soil and preparing the groundwork. I know it *sounds* lazy, but trust me, it's better to cultivate a relationship with a woman that is worthy of being in a relationship with you than try to transform her into relationship material.

You can't turn a whore into a housewife. There, I said it.

To avoid being dumped or burned by low-quality women, stick to your guidelines and communicate to her that YOU are the one who's trying to figure out if she's right for you. YOU are the man in this situation and being with a woman that adds immense value to your life is a TOP priority. You're not willing to settle for anything than the BEST.

But right now you're probably thinking…

"How do I make her chase me?"

Easy, MAKE her jump through a few hoops.

It's not being sneaky, it's being judicious about how, who, and what you spend your valuable time and energy on. As a high-quality man, you must learn to *appraise* the people, places, and things in your environment and make sound decisions on who and what is worth YOUR attention. So learn to make women jump through a few hoops to be with you, and you can do this best by following your guidelines.

For instance, in the preliminary stages of dating a woman, don't accept any excuses, cancellations, or run-arounds. In the intermediate stages of dating her, if you've been quite clear that you're looking for a long-term relationship and she doesn't want one, walk away. Become a master at weeding out women who are either not very interested in you or who don't meet your high, but reasonable standards.

Learn to say "No", and to feel good about it. Say it a few times right now out loud. Say it with your chest out. Yell the word if you want. Feels good doesn't it? Yeah, it should. When you're trying to find the RIGHT woman, learning how to say "no" will be your most powerful weapon for attraction.

Always lead a woman into the kind of relationship YOU want to cultivate. You lead, she follows. If she doesn't like it, walk away. And let's say you've found a phenomenal woman with amazing relationship potential. If so, when you feel the time is right, and you've assessed her worthiness, give her the gift of your full commitment.

But does she want your full commitment? Yes, she does.

Trust me, if you chose the right woman in the first place, she'll be the one trying to *catch you* for a committed relationship even while you're still assessing her value. The more interested she is, the less subtle she'll be about it. If you're dating a highly compatible and gorgeous woman who's so attracted to you that she wants you all to herself, you my friend, have a wonderful problem on your hands.

The Right Foundation For Relationship Cultivation

If you're a high-quality guy and you're trying to cultivate a relationship with a woman who's just not right for you, all your efforts will prove futile and you'll end up looking quite ridiculous. I can't stress this point enough. Finding the RIGHT woman in the first place is worth your time and effort, IF you value your sanity of course.

Any guy can learn how to attract a woman. It's not rocket science. Any guy can also learn how to "pick up women"; it's not astrophysics. But very few guys know how to attract a 'total package' woman that's right for them, and even fewer know how to KEEP her interested in them long enough to cultivate a great relationship.

The key to being in this small category of successful men is to filter out the women that don't match up to your guidelines. If she has the potential for a long-term relationship, the foundation is set and you can begin the cultivation process.

So the moral of the story is to be confident in what you want and to be satisfied with yourself as a man. Learn to be patient instead of being desperate. Always respect the women you come across, but ensure that they respect you as well. If a woman cannot respect you, you have NO USE for her.

Read that last sentence three more times before you move on.

Develop a powerful built in B.S. detector and learn to call people out on their crap. Get those who constantly mistake your compassion for weakness out of your life and take it as a lesson learned. And learn to laugh at your lessons in wisdom whenever they pop up in your mind.

Women will always seek out two things from a man: love and leadership, and not necessarily in that order. If a high-quality woman feels that you cannot lead her, she won't be able to love you. It's as simple as that my friend.

So instead of focusing on attracting a bunch of women that'll only waste your time and energy, work on improving yourself and broadening your horizons. Be authentic and candid with people, and expect the same. Find your path in life and stay on it, and place all of your energy on becoming a better man.

BONUS CHAPTER:
Making The List

The Right Questions

I've taken the liberty of adding this bonus section because I know for a fact that MOST guys who read this book are not going to follow through with making a list. I don't want YOU to be in that category so I'm going to make it even easier for you to define what it is you want in a girlfriend.

I've separated each of the questions into several categories to help you organize your thoughts and desires. So sit down someplace quiet with pen and paper and really give these questions some thought:

I. Physical Beauty & Appearance

What is her hair color?

What is her eye color?

What is her skin tone?

What is her body type?

What is her general height?

What is her sense of style?

II. Health & Fitness

What is her physical condition?

Does she workout habitually?

What kind of diet does she follow?

Is she energetic or more laid-back?

III. Money & Career

What is her approach to finances? Is she dependent, independent, or interdependent with a man?

Do you mind if she has debt? If yes, how much can you tolerate?

Is she a spender, a saver, or does she have a good balance?

Is she entrepreneurial or career/job focused?

What kind of accomplishments should she have?

Is she ambitious and career-oriented or simple and prefers to build a home and family?

IV. Family & Relationships

Is she more family-oriented or socially independent?

Is she very social, moderately social, or not very social at all?

How does she treat the men in her life?

Does she want marriage in the near future (1 – 3 years) or in the far future (3 years+)?

Does she have any children of her own? If so, how many?

What is her appetite for sex like? High, moderate, or low?

V. Spiritual Beliefs & Values

Does she uphold traditional views of male and female roles in relationships or is she more modern in her thinking?

What is her general outlook on life? Is she optimistic, pessimistic, or a realist? Which do you think you need?

What are her religious beliefs if she has any?

What kind of personal values does she have that are most important to you as a man? How would you describe her character?

VI. Skills, Talent, & Intellect

Is she ambitious or more modest in her life goals?

What kind of skills should she possess? Example: Good cook, athletic, good with children, etc.

Is she ambitious in her career or prefers to build a home and family?

Is she opinionated and steadfast in her thinking or open-minded?

VII. Passions, Hobbies, & Interests

What kind of hobbies should she be interested in?

Does she have similar tastes in music, movies, books, etc.?

Does she share your goals and your picture of an ideal lifestyle?

What things do I want her to enjoy doing with me?

After you feel that you've completely defined your ideal woman, be sure to write out your detailed description and place it somewhere that you can see it everyday. Think about your ideal relationship and how it would make you feel.

Dare to dream big, but be sure to go out there and begin meeting new women that fit your ideal description. Who knows? Maybe you might come across that one special girl that you want to spend the rest of your life with. Hey, if it happened to me it can happen to any guy.

About Bruce Bryans

Bruce is a successful writer, website publisher, and author. He has written many articles for various online publications and enjoys sharing the triumphs (and failures) of his love life with anyone who enjoys a good laugh or a life lesson.

When he isn't tucked away in some corner of his house writing a literary masterpiece (or so he thinks!), Bruce spends most of his time engaged in his hobbies or being a romantic nuisance to the love of his life. And after spending most of his twenties studying books about psychology, seduction, dating, and relationships, he's happy to finally have a gorgeous, exotic, sun-kissed goddess with a heart of gold to share his life with.

Best Books by Bruce Bryans:

Below is a short list of some of my other books that you can find on Amazon.com. Here's the link to my book list where you can access all of the books listed:

http://www.amazon.com/author/brucebryans

101 Things Your Dad Never Told You About Men: The Good, Bad, And Ugly Things Men Want And Think About Women And Relationships

In *101 Things Your Dad Never Told You About Men*, you'll learn what high-quality men want from women and what they think about love, sex, and romance. You'll learn how to seduce the man you want or captivate the man you love because you'll know exactly what makes him tick.

Attract The Right Girl: How To Find Your Perfect Girl And Make Her Chase You For A Relationship

In *Attract The Right Girl*, you'll discover how to find and choose an amazing girlfriend (who's perfect for you) and how to spark the kind of attraction that'll lead to a long-term relationship with her.

How To Get Your Wife In The Mood: Quick And Dirty Tips For Seducing Your Wife And Making Her BEG You For Sex

In *How To Get Your Wife In The Mood,* you'll discover the relationship secrets used by some of the most blissful couples in the world as well as romantic hacks that'll help you to get all the sex you want from your wife and make it seem like it was all HER idea.

How To Be A Better Boyfriend: Win Your Dream Girl's Heart, Master Her Emotions, And Keep Her Helplessly Attracted (And Loyal) To You

In *How To Be A Better Boyfriend*, you'll discover how to cultivate a rock-solid, mind-blowing, romantic relationship with your dream girl, and what to do to avoid all the drama, bad girlfriend (or wife) behavior, and game playing that many "nice guys" often fall prey to in relationships.

Meet Her To Keep Her: The 10 Biggest Mistakes That Prevent Most Guys From Attracting And KEEPING An Amazing Girlfriend

In *Meet Her To Keep Her*, you'll learn the ten dating mistakes that stop most guys from attracting and keeping a 'Total 10 girlfriend' and how to overcome them.

What Women Want In A Man: How To Become The Confident Man That Women Respect, Desire Sexually, And Want To Obey…In Every Way

In *What Women Want In A Man*, you'll learn how to become a high-quality, self-confident man that can naturally attract a good woman and keep her "well-trained" in a relationship.

Make Her Melt With Your Words: Romantic Things To Say And Text To Tease, Titillate, And Turn Your Wife On

In *Make Her Melt With Your Words*, you'll find out how to use hypnotic romantic phrases and sensual text messages to make your wife feel beautiful, adored, and sexually irresistible to the man she loves and desires.

13135848R00067

Made in the USA
San Bernardino, CA
10 July 2014